"When will Aunt Jane bring the pu
said Wendy. "I can't wait to pick out
new puppy!"

"Aunt Jane will be here in about two hours," Mother told Wendy. "You can help me with some things while we wait. A puppy needs good care, you know."

"First, a puppy needs something to eat from and something to drink from," said Mother. "Your puppy can eat from one of these and drink from the other."

"And a puppy needs a bed," said Mother.
"You can help me with this bed while we wait.
Then we can put it in your room."

"This is a good bed," said Wendy. "Will the
puppy have to stay on it all night?"

"Yes, it will," said Mother.

Next, Wendy ran out to see her father.

"I can't wait to pick out my new puppy!"

"Well, Aunt Jane will be here in about an hour," said Father. "You can help me with this doghouse while we wait."

"This is a great doghouse!" said Wendy. "The puppy can stay in it while I'm at school."

Aunt Jane came right on time. Wendy ran
to give her a hug.

"Mother and I made a bed, and Father and
I made a doghouse," Wendy said. "Can I pick
out a puppy now?"

"I do not think you have to pick out
a puppy," said Mother.

Father said, "I think your puppy has
picked YOU!"

Wendy and her new puppy played
for hours. They ran and jumped, jumped
and ran. Then they played and played
until it was time to come in to eat.

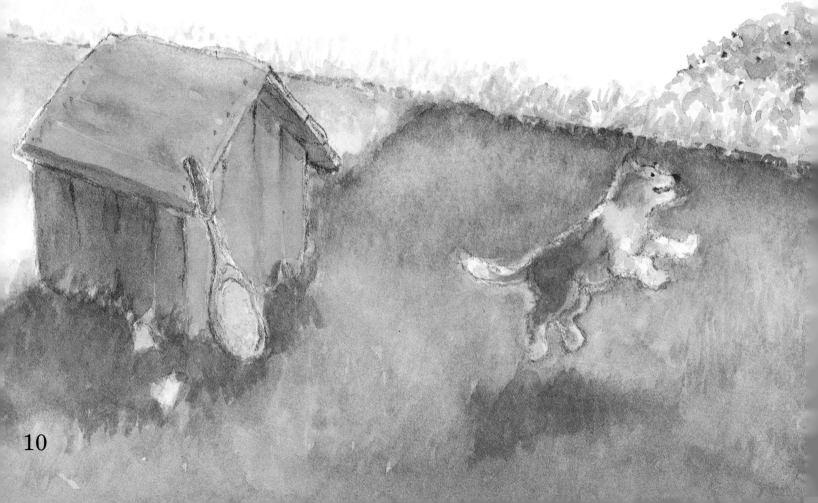

Mother showed Wendy how to give
her puppy food and water.

Then they all went out for a walk.

After that, Wendy and the puppy played
in Wendy's room for hours.

When night came, Father said, "We'd better tell Wendy that it's time for bed."

"It's very quiet in there, isn't it?" said Mother.

When Mother and Father went to Wendy's room, they had a big surprise.

14

Wendy was not in her bed. The puppy
was not in its bed. There were Wendy and
her puppy sleeping on the rug!

"Now we know why it was so quiet
in here," said Father.

"It's quiet now," said Mother, "but just wait until morning!"